Shaler's Fish
POEMS

HELEN MACDONALD

Shaler's Fish
POEMS

Atlantic Monthly Press
New York

Published in association with Etruscan Books, UK

Published simultaneously in Canada
Printed in the United States of America

FIRST EDITION

ISBN 978-0-8021-2463-0
eISBN 978-0-8021-9070-3

Atlantic Monthly Press
an imprint of Grove Atlantic
154 West 14th Street
New York, NY 10011
Distributed by Publishers Group West

groveatlantic.com

15 16 17 18   10 9 8 7 6 5 4 3 2 1

*When I sat me down before my tin pan, Agassiz brought
me a small fish, placing it before me with the rather stern
requirement that I should study it, but should on no
account talk to anyone concerning it, nor read anything
related to fishes, until I had his permission so to do.*

—Nathaniel Southgate Shaler, *Louis Agassiz as a Teacher:
Illustrative Extracts on His Method of Instruction, 1917*

Contents

SHALER'S FISH

SAFETY CATCH

Taxonomy

Wren. Full song. No subsong. Call of alarm, spreketh & ought
damage the eyes with its form, small body, tail pricked up & beak like a hair

trailed through briars & at a distance scored with lime scent in the nose
like scrapings from a goldsmith's cuttle, rock alum & fair butter well-temped

which script goes is unrecognised by this one, is pulled by the ear
in anger the line at fault is under and inwardly drear as a bridge in winter

reared up inotherwise to seal the eyes through darkness, the bridge speaks
it does not speak, the starlings speak that steal the speech of men, *uc antea*

a spark that meets the idea of itself, apparently fearless.
Ah cruelty. And I had not stopped to think upon it

& I had not extended it into the world for love for naught.

Morphometry

I have had live crows, hawks, owls, opossums, squirrels, snakes and lizards so that my own room sometimes reminded me of Noah's ark; but Noah had a wife in one corner of it and in this particular our parallel does not altogether tally.

Alexander Wilson

I had an idea of this, is stacked with song
& cool blood, bruised with salad herbs & oil
Of petrae, callt oil of peter, salts, flats, larks.
Wet feathers continue to rise in my breast
Whereas your darker plumes operate a weak tacet
broken in twain, *se muer,* to moult & speak for a hope
For a moment or two for the pile of the land rocks back
in a dubitable movement shiny as a climate sere
As desert, it is all flush. Through a miracle of hatred
an expansion of range will serve, as light in itself;
Light and even as absolutely nothing else is.

But not wanting to wander across interior spelts
inclined to bruise it as the pelf of good fortune, love.
To rack the head with love. A removeable locus of bloody
and clouded leaves is politic & linear upon that phrase
Weighing classically so that the thought forgets itself
with difficulty. At once removes a tiny sphinx of tin
a shy and discreet creation, doubtless fussed by thin shadows
of bent sinew & pneumatised bone, my heart wilted in them

Home. Some miracle of hatred brought forth an expansion of range.
Nothing as durable as something which otherwise might take leave
soar up into a sky trailing wax and bells and subsist on its own.
It broke into something resembling a plan of submission;
grackles redrawn in the margin, and the whole arched
in pilasters of massy cloud. Doubt not but that the dead
were torn by the vision, where no place lies, there is none
to be had. In truth none at all, not even the aspiration to,
believing it spring and the heart it had sprung from dead.

Poem

Take a voice you know only
spliced, known as Pantagruel
and shut in a clasp of warm rose.
An elegiac feathering of black
singes the wood and imagines
a ludic impasse, I mean to
nothing you meant. And two
distances to demonstrate
an oratorial distress, by sight
who you might not ever calm
or comb out of mind, *might,*
leaning a little heavy on
suchlike benevolence pressing
a keel to my hand
and all the weather
prating it, yours as a gift.
I am in England.
There are rings on my brow.
　　　　This is a friend.
That is a show of fire pinned
to the lapel's politic dart siring
the one with the ivory face, some
downy conjunction spun into blue, this is
too too a friend, whose open word carries
the land away, the heart flying strongly
to sea.

Blackbird/Jackdaw/
Turdus/Corvus/merula/monedula

So. A spire pulled forward by gravity of anger into limes
brief ripple of disc-shaped serrated leaves & lineage

dropped into a ladle at dusk as swifts spit softly
overhead in lines from physics and buttons

slate, where it falls and falls. Battalions of heroes eh.
That is what we schemed to hear. Walls of them, with bad

luck on their side. What a curious pose you are holding
spare hopes for certainty she does, the heroes touch leaves

to their foreheads as they walk it is May, May damp May
on gravel.

Résistant à toute pression sans casser

Halfway through the
sequence the rose
spluttered I *went* out

of house &
home this broody thou
connest dealing *only*

filled with dulcet oil. Have
you sent for me laughing
have you spoke in the exquisite

revisionary hearing arc. Delta
put a siege in here for exhumation
forgot, forgot.

It implausible.
no. avoidance of forms
for her personal history
clear bands

East/Absence of heat

Wake, in a room where soft plaster has fallen
& coercion sets itself pastimes, very sure of itself
bringing a little light into our world and then some
sessile cast of light seems meticulous in its suffering
the very notions of welfare and well-being themselves

perfunctorily stropped as a beak or a blade
folding the light back to the chest where it frays
in soft genuflections of denomination and rescue.
One of the most beautiful, figuratively speaking propositions is tired of you
& all I can do is concur with a real figure of speech, you move, you die.
In doorways apostrophising is acceptable currency

It's fine. We have time. There is a vault within safety
square as a bean's stem & the ocean pushed both ways from it,
a parting of the waves which is musical and which sings to secure me,
& spare as the keel I would fly over it, if I could, being sport.
The days have lain to secure me. My hands follow. Those eyes

I draw on walls and squares of tape are plainly mine, whose
patterns divine themselves for securement. The day has lain
to secure me & drives itself blind towards night in its haste
for securement. I am but a latch with it, & its comfort lacked.
I fear the laying on—wait on—a little flush in my eyen hath bruised me.

No small collapse but aptitude, itself an interest
forc'd like flowers, and such is education.
Which is that line again.
Which seems incurable. Curare in the eye
And so the form cut out by means of sympathy.

Section VIII

Any idea is sufficient for the purpose you understand
this offensive on bright lines as bringing distinction

to militant bliss . . . all counter to what I deserve.
Can you tell what it is? Is it subservient to a wish

for deliberation, for a fine incision to split the junction
boxed so the lights go pop in a deal of amphoteric

glitter? Or dual clinker to fill the peace process
with incidental crimes; this is where gazes fit

and splinter rhymes from kit and kin and strip
the rest as if shopping. It is becoming clear.

Now, except at particular times, I do not think
it affects at all . . .

. . . huge indiscretions laying down an evening
for premeditated warmth and rescue . . .

running on though some lines were cut
simply to preserve the shadow of the impassive

& well, it's something to feed on
breaking crockery and trefoil for clover, so

engaging a manner that snaps
not that its extraordinary emotions have any

connection with positive pain.

Hyperion to a Satellite

At 6:55 the morning opened: *pax non*
for a papery drawl & a bolt of free fire, a metalled

glimmer and a fireball, some shallow
and luminous winter cloud dropping tektites

of Island Heritage in steep iterative waves
no sympathy furled to surface ice approximates

Widmanstatten's grating pat, with a formula
of primitive and suitably drenched olivine. Noble metals

are dropped onto accident blackspots, hailing
from districts of open light, glossing the connectives

with a discriminating solar bombardment, and not
that the radio grooves to the busiest man on the beeb

& his twenty questions strook there shimmering
on the road to fame, planning one's life

around the form to say, nearly 5000 companies
across Europe. And a video-entry system.

This plate of diamonds is older in gravure.
City air curves to the critical point and the function

plots as something neat and gravid: parcels
of ephemera, bands of travertine and portland stone.

Touchy subject, but a nice, even object.
One side was polished in encouraging chronology & so on-

ward to a field of blue ice, pitted with rain
& chivalry, indices bleeding all over the page

rotating right or left as the man says—some
thing's got to give or get said in a trice with

some cloud's dusty emancipation—and thus
a material gain slightly embarrassed in a deal

hedge, still nice, & still warm to the touch.

Parallax Nonpareil

How did Newton, his 1676 discovery, aid our perception of colour?
Shall we apply his own theoria to a bunch of several lines
two bridges over the English Countryside involving moons
a little rushing water & a biddable theme: means to live
sweet as a die, & die sweetly into 10-space: how many
shadows there, on that shape? For a basic education?

There must be a place for EACH.
& if integrity softens, reckons itself
to be DEFT, kindness in parallel
then revenge is sweet. But being asked [at length]
to ALTER; as if whatever magnificent traffic
intends from its period stance a light, the cast
parries fashionable cuffs with an aimiable use of those terms
qua love, call the stave's cause my rejection.

Nowhere near the gentle westerly slope
is listing the recent case a dream for consideration
of sorrow and origins, mistaking the gait for home.

Small Hours

There is a brick in the cloud
               but it is not falling
it is night falling
is it true accomplishment breathing

The sky isn't blue not thinking
for days thinking for you

generally a small kind of bird looking
for premises
and they say the best is, yet
                   to get near it
requires such fabric of years there is a
stroke through it
& I can stand on the pantomime wall
describing figures.

And above
a splint of mild lightness that is not
light at all that is all there is to love

Phosphorous

The curb is dead; half one hour
at the hospital gates with versions

corollary: the beautiful insulatory
properties of the English Channel

waning with imitative desires, wounds
at best shedding operative phraseology

along the coast, some hydrous shimmer
of silica and humorous mettle; love

in the mouth. He sorts her throwaway
lines & shouts in a fumy kind of translucent push

as demonstrations of thisness mesh into black-
edged letters and slated rings. If someone

or other inmate trembles this sleeping mean
to the manner of Davy's beautiful ice, not

wanting to replicate the dubious conditions
despite the need for water—when three

elevens construct a scalar height, one on one
to view the drift of a popular song & climb

to take the swarm from the sleepers breadth
then longing folds all fields to bright lines

and broadcasts heavy bunching too.
such a beautiful delivery as a war is.

Sympathy

One of you is counting for cover & recovery.
You are recovering, not doubting the necessity
for succinctness and/or an elusive personal worry.
But the crowds get so terribly near the sea, and clouds
of inky pyrethrum shearing petrel wings free of lice
petals gripping the teeth of both world wars as *semblant,*

a kind of *gott natur* on canvas. But your drift, chattering on
in this manner with a grout effigy of safety: whether showed
or shown or sewed into rage is strategy for starters.
You will never finish the half of it. And the question
for stars is a revered negative swept across the frontage
of the drowning cities, all safe now from care

now *there* was a historical synthesis that we had a hand in
floating ships across the tangentially heating blues; but these
were not seas, but successions of use and privation,
easing rain upon canopies, cracking gold into shale
in your delicate search, your halcyon dream
of void fortune

love seems to inform the truer statements as statuary
& here I am in rhapsody vis-a-vis that *rara avis*
of reasonable beauty. Shingle moves
the seasons presume a delicacy of touch
& the position is light: a casual vacancy
one moot point. clean. in a void of blocks and secrecy

Poem

Bright the what, reins wherever you go something
keeps at the forefront & might this be a while here
rest a little, see how easy the land fits like a lamp
the hand as it keeps, small fowles pruneth

rain runs from their backs in nomadic immortality
holes for each eye, pygostyle, furcula, pinions oiled
& the grease directs neat beads from throat chat chat
hatching barbs and sills broken white as a flint egg

bright the sight, I joked & slept
seeing the words run together like quick
the sky was also spilt; my coat it ran upon
was caught & soaked; the air afire with light

through mist, the very perfect, gentle night
an asterisk in the vacancy where should stand the sun
trawling the air downwards & laced with vehement calm
that lattice of stems admixed with leaves in butter.

the sound of thunder, claps of thunder, & hay, waning.
the thunder rolling about the air in differentials, the air
a slick & referential: portrait and landscape, scape and sore
a hough cut like that, trees swinged and crashed with vernal fire

where the sere and drouth is stood & picking strings out
of ligament, music. Try a distance off, listening with care
trust as amused as an arm open to sensate pleasure
the land is falln over.

Hand to Mouth

Turning back from the conservatory wall, buries
his head in a nest of black hamburg vine & smiles but once
as the leaves tremble, the shine holding a gun loaded
with brief papers, that little winter held in the mind
just a visitor, as little winds will throw catterns out
& tiny red anthems do foster themselves in March.

To hurt the eyes a delit in troubled scourings
of glass, gardens hardly there but in a cup of blank
scratchings and fosse to see him stir and shriek, but
cannot; is maled up upon a cushion, and set there
where the fire bloweth, and the sparkes jet up and down.
This is the best way to bring him to familiarity.

Which shoulder is troubling you? Which is leant
against the thirty brickes on the water, the wall
& breaking in sunder the inquiry of love? Apparently
no order but hee should have him by the necke, and we
are all well pleased, it is great oddes he will no further.
But whiling here, by the straight line of the river, where

we shall bury him; it is love or leaves, the locus abandoned.
Small fowles picketh themselves in drops, and wilted drops
and falls of song. And after, we may to the champion; once
out into the plaine we. And the real dislike, as a street
of pale clouds converge on the town, that nature
is drawn unto the lives of men.

Nash

That broad light spills on fallow land
that ink is soft & spurred with leaves and combes
That parse of wonderment extends in flints and barres
a match for wings a lapse, *lusus ingenii* and love

Which reaches up to buff a tan page with water
& pigment a wall of the Battle of Britain with ire.
Sour teak, wet light & a saw to roughen up an edge
or weaken it in a clasp of weak pink cloud/a rose.
A sufficiency of roads and caritas, of canvas slept in
motley, unusual weeping, maternal commas,
national fervour collapsed.

You knew they might dislike these greys
burnt metals who slip from thermals, Kings,
Hamiltons, darker papers roasted with clouds
to a beached Blenheim on the Caspian coast,
suave altars of colour, dealt cross after cross
for weak lungs, weak feet, weak arms.

Now glassy tiles subject the road to stress
for reflections' wake, a burn that classes piecemeal
clause as 'oration's own great calm.' And all is lost.
Sward is grown again and a black
covert plume is blown from the dead bird's back.
What ethics frame, & flue outwardly 'the realm of nature'
is a rubric fine enough to scrape or panell inwardly & result in zero

and I am thinking where my eye is

Poem

for Bill Girden

Death, about which we are all thinking, death, I believe
is the only solution to this problem of how to be able to fly
                              Paul Nash, *Aerial Flowers*, 1945

To state the discovery of a country
& be in a time without rage, keeping wings
near yourself, as barred as buried in the day, crossly.
Some present results; a tree, a quail, a rock, a hawk
rousing one's mind from safety and tameable illness
to beautiful comprehension in the form of a hunch
as patience directs

the finishing line is a trail of feathers to brush.
You might resist the pall of earthly wings
wicker thrumming with sand and hysteria
no longer a word, no use, knocking at wind
or poise as it flows up along the face, an edge
clipped with rock and lifting, a movement

as if one were about to launch into speech of faith
at least a hoped conviction, spite of coincidence.
'This is hardly a flaw; it simply is' you say, then drop
like a lark in abeyance of song to mitigate sward.
My pen crumples into a swan, it is singing
inauthenticate myth, and not of future splendour

I am glad. Some evidence of a hymn without light. Fracas.
History. The building of a condominium.
It was true I had never met.
There was a strike on the glass; it was a bird.
I have never been to the desert.

Tuist

I

Pleat the grounds they have scripted
as such, plus plumage, quiet lunches
on the hotel lawns slipping forward
'til we sense some dutiful square
and stop, pulling the whole rueful shore
to a ha ha, a net around practical ankles
      ah, how the hay smokes
into papaverous skies
as we address the heights of the C20th
in a poplin shirt, all declamatory and tired
with a suit that seals to rest these soft
and perfect metals. The organisation
owes everything; is fit to tweak
a neuralgic scene reading Auden
beneath a naked sheet in stormy cupolas
where the coupled latch and larchlap twitter
breaks sleet print through the cigarette
dries trays of warm roses & vocable ash
as hands permitting a multiple
sleepless walk for the uninked signatory
through august hours, the graces
who imagined that body of angels
and the debt before news, or words
as arms at the imprecise station

whose aim I cannot choose, being
a directive of squares
and breeze, tunnelling beauty
recovered & squired for the journey
briefly thumbing the air or worse
peripatetic squirms, nerves in nature
identical colours. That name at the firm
window is working effacement, soft gaps
and abstracted pairs to replace a miraculous
                       slang with cramp
reparation of gifts and speech in repose
over waving clouds and malt skeins
a salt cheque, bruised with an isolate nuance
where the girl in the hand is worth two
in the lunular dust, supposing
a plus might emerge in the dark like a mouse
dyed strawberry blonde, a russet cup
with leavened blue stretches, a blue
from the bolt to cut that darling crop:
black light amounts to a bulb, the map
is a cognitive station amounting to dark
as a matter of course, brings
theories of crisp summer use
to be closed on the family hearth
that book beneath another burns
in birds and stipes a human heart
pricking out heartsease and fumitory
whose Troy, etc., and an operatic tremble
thinning widthways on powdery wires,
should kiss the choir searching for water
                    & seasonal coyness
funnelled up in the glistening hide
for comparable pleasantries. Hereby

some clouds drag above motion, dry
windward with westerly lime & hang
their dripping heels with music;
this surfeit proposes a well apart
from softness and leverage; songs
to stall and wake. A personal
historical waive is planning to do so;
steal a face slams a song in my heart.

II

several lines to make
a linnet who did not know whether
he was a bird or no sleep
in a cupboard grows to slake
practice trills with a rattle
of fire

III

What means this, but soft
as a winged quail on turf [glut]
several spots of aeruginous blood
[but for] an accent, perfect
as a swerve from congeries to fear
from nothing to fear, from flood [damn]
to recoil from the heard response
& its demonstrable superfluities
to demolish the rails amidst [kilter]
recurring spoils in the eyes, to stand
on any difficult mountainside [again]
and the manner of features
the mutable hammers [reprises]

IV

Or mimics sleep to sleep
and so sleeps all for love
where a voice parades a handsome
faux-naïf on stones. Clinker, clink clink
binoculars trained on Maeterlink, the
headland, the bobolink and the lyre

a great light I don't know over land nor sea
is colouring fires, looking down on the spilt lyric
to create the corporeal panegyric amid waste
peregrinations of speech and, so far as any
limit blushed with the weight could I get
an urban syllogism stapled in there yet

it was better now. With a rope
ladder falling from the golden
bough, warmly engrossed & gone
to seed legislature, she showed
anew great prescience, relaxing
in to enormous strictures, shuttling

miles out & up into fearsome
clouds whose lapse rate reaches
for calm. *Enter spring*
water & dreamt calculations
burned on the chest, since the least
whistle curling away from speech

where a helpful confluence of air
and alula sends accuracy up from its perch

in golden scales and cries *oriole* for rainbird

Simple Objects

Not to touch the glare that breaks, and climate,
broaching the heart
with a talisman of salt. What hurt could be poured

to a glass and swung to see the bells of heaven ringing
for my procurement. A possible scratch sets me free

Of the modern, hear & fir mystery
to something I have to spell with no

nation, ankle deep in the mark, fretless
mirage radiant and anxious to settle

not least in the ambient glare. Catalogue me
where safety fits an evening outline, soldiers

firing at silver & the fringe of the pale sky
a conference of dotage, dying into the arctic

*   *   *

Caritas hijacked, music pulled in there, scent
erased in the deep temperature. Gauze follows

the return of an observation at a lines' end
soaked with flint and knocked by reddish sympathy

music sweats acres of slight and damaged inches
squared by the arc and protection of open water

but just to miss it, by this much, slapped
by plastic, and the press gathering toward

a hand of violets and cirrus hacked
backward to the infinite recession

of philosophy; that cloudy horizon
formulae of classic narcoses.

*　　*　　*

Act after act the spate is overdone
in a pyrrhic dusk, though the narrowing

of both eyes seems perfectly attained;
making mouths from the glass

white sleight of viper and file
whose past becomes a logic

spliced to itself and limited
only by the pressure encoded

at the neck's back. Putting
brevity at the angle of heel

and lake, halcyon days to pleat
in crape and claimants, all of them

felt and left and dressed in tactical red, readily
touched by high voices and a chancery dance

which whitens charcoal & leans hush against harm
so the throat broadens into song

* * *

here we are again
happy as can be
all good pals &
jolly good company

never mind the weather
never mind the rain

we weather tragedy
but the weather
is not tragic

off we go again

* * *

Material where the gallows
pillow & silence is

where the cloud gets
to fetch light & matter

meaning not a minute
waiting for a morning

I am alone and calm
beneath the juggled volumetrics

of hope and russian vine
minting water in a tier

of modest cause

to put the word here
where the mind was.

Occlusion of light
and sound left a space

for the matter, mere
havoc. At last, the token

gesture of trust. A grey space
uninhabited by fuss

*   *   *

Thereupon a nerveless mention, & through it
the tensile maceration of a copse-bound wind

hard enough to scrape four walls together
& wind up belaboured with years

uncomplicate in a heap the years lie
uncomplicate in a heap

SHALER'S FISH

the new world

Memetics are mute phylogenies and smarting.
What is a hand for, but to be held? It is raining

in Georgia it is raining all over the world
applause rattles from the pilot's beak in choppy

breves & *savoir faire* lost somewhere between here
and home where the heart is whatever. The light

is hard in departures & tightness of the chest harder
weak toxicologies the accents of the dreams aren't murder

scene after scene ships demeanour with trade
sets a leaving tear on each cheek & fades

and says: this is a real blade, fifteenth century, Japan.
Or: a peculiarly Germanic form of armour, no holes for eyes

black all over, annealed, the frayed corporeal manner
as the mouth sups grounds, faults and folds the arms under

but the shade of your eyes approximates the blade's blued dorsal edge
indigent as the model's side or even air, seen from below

every moment describes some other music
and I cannot remember banality ever existing

Dale

The storm runs forth on several seas whose manner is
the hard edge of a clamber down gneiss with a split thumb
huge inklings of wonderment, sun and trenchant killing bumped
by wrecked spume and clearing the throat, to try and shout
into the wind. Pulled out like warm glass. Where should flight

Eight choughs and three children, singing to a seal's head
on the lee side of the cliffs, hair fraying, *he-lo, he-lo* diatomite
and rain, disyllabic chuckle as the corvids glean turf and turn downwind
pealing back a sheet of egyptian cotton new/vraiment class
bled into a strong silence, just equalled by watching

Thirty breakers cowling in diagrammatic vice-lines with shortening frequency
replaced by thirty more/the ferry aspect two miles out dimmed by light
in cloud and rolls of clean water scrolling down. There are fits of waking.
I am waiting, it seems, for the cliff's right edge, but it is turned down
into a fence: slack barbs in hubs and shelves of thrift. Nothing sells

Nothing sells about this edge but fragrance, when the eyes are closed
enough to tip the head away from the ledge and settle it in welsh mud
'this is how the Irish write, as if with their left hand' she said, as soft
as anything, and the frown was half-sustained astonishment, looking
out across the waves as if a clause, then down at the paper in my hand

Nothing as matter as fact as dislike occurs either here or for other places
as worn, something to get to. I could hurry by in a parsimonious cinch
frosted umbellifers and wagtails in the flat wastes ankle-deep in water
thinking how it got here and confusing this with national history:
natural history arches its timbre uncomfortably: nine races of *Motacilla*

flava, four of *alba*, victorious identification through chalk and paste
sliding eastwards on the vicious gradients come the disorientated:
twelve with a broken neck beneath the light and scores in bushes
on the wrong wind for this bird, a miracle behind glass
discarded on reflection

Have Blue

Metal grows warmer against the skin
such implications of expediency call this realism

projected as an interior difficulty, of apprehension
blown past as a sere white line over the desert index

a forefinger held up to the sky could see it, but for lack
of noise unloaded at night since the presupposition of a target

costive pitch and yaw or roll corrected by wire like water
falling all around him with cosine squeals the line rolled up

and light also fell into it. Like wine dark. Sees elsewhere
in disks of water and a rapid participatory grace

elements of predation holding the eye & not without risk
this grace, a candour tipped to cede darkness with order

an aeolian matte stripped as soft as the image of breath
bronze against bronze where the cupped hand

plenty falls. A fox sparrow shadow on blue stone
broke diamond cut cuticle where rain pools schematics

of the calm scintillarions of a falling sky
and the porous wind of a little country

the steep inklings of the tongue's tip
& the implications of a mountain buried in snow

these are lambent philosophies requiring water
new marks to which the mouth is an applied science

Jack

where diviners are hauling water is a bump of turf
and a cloud caul low over old heather scurf, sleep.
Dodder wrapt and a mimic fit to klepe greenshank
cotton blowing eastward, a match-mime set in as ore
shoulders sunk, heavy as rain and thistlewool merlin
blinking at the roll of weather. New roles settle, ticking
gently at the pitch and yaw singing out an arc overland

a whisper of suspicious music like the stars are dead
and the real fact of succession is dripped over rock in a sincere bid
to stay. But there is no stay. There is ice at the steady damage
patterned ground and small burrows where air laps and falls
an emergency environment at the instant where the jack comes
parabellum of delicacy and mores

violent spoils as manuscript through drier air
manifest as movement

the video slips & marshalled antics fade

On approaching natural colours

The elegy of the bough is turned to earth
turns as a blister. Three tillers have formed. It is dry.

That straight line doth not contain everything I know
& everything I have not yet understood. It is not an is,

nor a cline not a bar, a predicament. The parliament
of fowls & the wheel of clouds, clouds' sake

Where it sickens again, meaning to place it for hours
& an ill wind picks at heroism, as a fence of flowers

against charms, charm. Ah, but you do suffer charm
who has suffered from the same & not proudly.

If the lips are mute then the claim is yours
something to baffle irrigation with, like sand

The bird is banked with earths & starts for cover.
Take a greate texte-penn and run for same.

Crickets scratch and burn beneath bracken & forms wither
and soak into waves through the optics of sunken light in summer

the water seethes, a tip burned into the wood hinges & hops in scales
of unlikely brilliancy; a patch of growling leaves, scalloped by wormes

Hard data secured in the systematics; one plus and the other
the rest burned off or cordoned into the emblematic eye

the mode for pernicious transcendence
Motifs to sweeten as pie. Such a book

made up as if to remark upon the eye
as of a rock, or the door is shut as

the rock falls, the plant extends into form
and driving it out in feathers the bird

spoiled later with 'first of all' and the wink still supple to void 'all those years'
demaquillage of the view so whet the schemata/a weak metachronal tick

through naphthalene and barley, looking upwards
the coil of singed aire, complexities pushing southeast

its particles fall: versions of love unconcerned with life:
let the wind renege & the fields upturn to sky

Route down

What could it be, it's a miracle
You're scheming on a thing that's sabotage
and absent from the scene even before it takes my leave
muttering portfoliate mirabelle, rococo launches out
stabilised wt. reference to the terminal's outer curve,
some favours granted by repute, though greeting is beyond
a momentary thought, ill suit: that fund who loves
safe spectres of pronounced abandon is clear
once again, both hands in choleric papers.

Dying defined as restitution gets to be stuttered
in a shock blackout where bass shook the vehicle
softly, now, recognising the intransigent kiss
of light pulled higher up the building's brownstone
fat arc willing the sun to descend faster, and it does
running glass upward to a couple of larus gulls
wandering about, tin-eyes flicked by nictitating
membranes this way and that coil and glide down
the harbour six miles to the east through sulphur

why in the city is
possibly illegal/in an ethical sense
anything over 800ASA a plausible danger, apparently
but forgiveable. Waiting around as if in a dream tapping
the foot watching the date flicker on the c-card
scrolling through an escape route, detailing the watch again
inspecting the mutable stitching holding him politely in time
symptomatic of an olivaceous return to the sobbing throat,
asphalt. Though the way I saw it, more of a threat. Just tactics,
love but mobile. Customs with static. Warm wars, buoying you along.
Small clauses derive an entire dream from a fit of chemical resilience
the click of the vendors sleek side and the rubble-roll of filled plastic
perfect under striplight and big oranges and CNN's indubitable grief

Enseamed

In this symbolic badinage
a lost cast of a single hour

waxes lyrical, like a bandage
around the head or a lyre

some anonymous foreign powers
planting a star where queues

form and recede for rejection.
Though a rout threatens to speak

the silks empty themselves only with love
& a black inch spreads feet-first from the thumb

on roads whose tonnes were hillsides
whose tunnels were hillsides

the heart is past it
its boring, beautiful light

Mine

the aim is fine tune gradual
the peace of heavy rain is owned
blinked to set resuscitation of vision
flashes of brilliance distant, maybe recede

he is carrying dust, and his certainty was
no-one wished themselves to accompany him
dismissing the ground as level, discussing
its ease of use. No, we will not hurt.

The ground will fade into beauty as easily
and the hasp of the air with lead
as the figure of one who is carried by another
sand blowing through the wide, broken streets

where frames are weak near the ocean
warm grey air slides up the riverine edge
condensing on the grains, making them cohere
the figures persevere as differences in structure emerge

distortions in vision induced by the sun
we could call them mirages rather than justifiable
blunders of suspense. Now the figure is moving
and we deduce his plan from our own; under stands of palm

the rattle of darkness held in *pandanus* rags
hardly seems possible this pool here, brilliant calm
is walking towards it, as if every imagined harm
discarded the tiny surface tension of chlorinated

warm blue and left it alone, the weakest thing
peeling from the surface in long chains by the sun
plotting the destruction of some moment & time
movement, or its creation, the same

witnessing the arc of evaporative calm
watching the sand, the witless climb
the moving pool, the waterfall of glass
sun below fire, the returning man

Walking

Where. Why and etcetera. The head bows & nothing is.
Shielding the harm from further harm is harder than this.
Voile & velux and little owls calling through dawn
mate selection, early spring on ash fence, white dots
a clave dancing sweetly on the posts. Not a call to arms
but I'm shaking anyway, and the sweet dawn is when
the wind gets up, half past four, cold on my face in the barn
in the sense of a register only: still alive, still hurt, whatever.

I am valorous in the face of such kindness, as ravens on pylons
stock doves and the roll of limestone bulks out our version
ripping out a throat in even dreams, eyes shut & breathing
concentrating on the sodden lake of the heart, and its sharp depths
up for retching on sweetness: sugar, tunes, airs, the memory of love

And a regular life. Where calm comes is never known, either
for the variety of declensions appal. Such a simple action alone
displacing a number of primary concepts, as trust and kindness
to dust, water: a lake of sweet cloves and lotus & the wind from the east
draining the land into raw salt and a poverty of sand and judgement
and I am balanced on one foot, assuming the next step is groundward
but wherever the ground is, blood.

Variations on Morphometry

Letter by letter, oxidised rag, cp. *Agrippa*, stance:
Koday, Kodaly, Lorenz, Lucretius. The Club of Rome

trawling black pages with a three ml border
lapsed adhesion, solid flowers pressed to same

where is the adult? Deictic pins and a shadow mazarine
drinking beside the pond 'Arthur on Dixie' likewise 1919

making in legal, might as easily be the record's blued edge
the hush of good suppression, tarnished ammunition

beneath a woodpile, or a strawhide implementation
bright marks of lands & grooves running down to the frieze

under the ledge at four degrees water in concrete & plywood
talc beneath the platform at the Norfolk and Western

hiking out to the shale pit, running ten dollars through
locking the hint back to lines from the Port Authority

knocked open the cinderblock and extended the magazine
cleaning the eye with three fingers and force of majority

bringing it all back home; the plan fashioned like water
two containers, an electrical charge, oxygen and fire

a fundamental indicator of health. Blink to miss
the revolutionary hope, the set suits, & it is symmetry all over

which silence revoked
the score wet, the lyre broke

Poem

For Roger Langley

flint is a colour & a hard thing as thinking is not
knowing what bothers the year shaking itself out
one black brant amongst palefronts the coast is wet
the fields are dry the fields are spring the sea is not

partly statuesque, partly a broken baroque tacet
scratched from the coast, an ode in particles
lifting the foot to sleep, no talk
no longer a war, just air

tiredness gone auratic hangs like a fuzzy
scientific cloud of derivatives about the head
the starlings have ceased to rain
like Shakespearian arrows/the ruin of france
an intrigue of variety when the head hurts

The palearctic eye. Sweet water. Where calm whet
sport in a scart line round the heart, street line
of practice and real good humour. Small
white flowers. Descant with a hammer.

Scaup red stone & blue bay out to Skokholm
a blued alcoholic gravitas inclining to alkalinity like
a dip of the head flows between stacks
p.o.v. widening to include the dissolve

discrete hatching to flat
white/despotic rock, clear
stub of mink in a linear panoply
linotype, gaussian blur, rotring black

there was a tune or a turn and a gait like walking
tweaked so that the fine line, thrip-fine shrugged off
admirably as powder, a mouth of water
asked to respond equitably to air

Don Quixote

Opening the set piece exotically, as if in the attempt
he could make it his own. A tinnitus of affect, that poise
shade and angled to shine on a few rich phrases
the western edge of his range. I loved this, though
criticism was beyond me, I felt it in my heart

A set or so later, more like a natural threat.
Poor discussions rescued by silence. Glitter of phosphenes
as I descended the stairs through a tunnel of wet paper
rain falling from the lintel inside and recognised it
whether I held it inside or out, as cut too close

Grazing distance, satisfied by the auratic hasp of a face
already casting about for other countries thus defended
when each breath lessens and less will bring it back
a fervour applied like a gift, he said never to think of it
as anything like anything he'd ever thought before

so which is more open now, above or below
when open land is a show of nothing at all. Clips, thins
and migrates, the wind dictating where the body falls
to what ends, and cools into a capacity of cryptic abandon.
He broods also on the work half-finished, his timetable

delayed with desire quenched here and there with sobriety
reconsideration and slower musicality patching up the season

but nothing reveals the precipice: where there is a wall
someone is underneath, kicking at stones, eating well
and describing something like memory.

Polymorphism be damned, no-one cares to speak of it
a deepening hint of editorial silence in a hired home
the telephone's electromagnetic silence *the stars are dead*
drummed out on the shortwave radio next door

old rhyme so soft it is likely inaudible
as the shift of the fall is likely unfeasible
as the previous heart is unrecogniseable
seeping magnolia in a wide swathe of notes
a little heart is steeped up, blind, bathed
in an amanuensis of salt.

I am here, I presume, the tables tell me so
where perfect consequence coughs in the middle of the song
and the air is good here, its excellent softness reminiscent of spring
piles of moulted feathers and charred elytra on slate, further
dreams of childhood houses and hard oak doors, partners

pouring tea from a height and sores on the backs of their hands
blooming with bright, light-deprived seedlings through autumn.
Linden leaves carpet the floor of the house and a warbler full-
throated in the hall, whose walls are weakened and cool
dismissing distress several times a second & returning anew

amity in the air as the garden is burned
and from this height the smoke is an occasion of beauty

Hitman.doc

There is no bravery involved in recognition
existentialisms final take on globalising statements/communism
your perfect petit object/control/decision/concert/honest
derision/concentrate on the point the point reached
not some sixties version of cool/St Tropez
hitman reads Merleau Ponty disassembling
the .22 conceit: a curio. *Lobster 27–36* on the table
knowing that sort/where to cease a soft target
musical thoughts on a heart/shot for the afternoon

at the denser edge of the room a figure is sometimes walking
sometimes writing aware of the time and where it is looking
an elementary sophism something to chat to like dreamers do
glass of Margaux reviewing the celerity of looks *Das Abenteuer*
dating an identity so precisely lenticular rubble spilt out along the floor
these people may have been clouds, they exhaled so precisely.
Dreaming of the spice of life. Proviso: mock
carbonates, bicarbonates, blocks of new snow

Named, and getting closer, a stamp at the far right
upper edge of the foolscap paper set up nights'
vanishing point bright on the opposite wall
& both hands closed on the gun in the mirror
anyone can buy a smile an elementary cloud chamber
which opportunity blocks, yet when morning comes as it does
you are still breathing, one hand on the frame

stretching the map cross the room where specific objects deform
its fabric down, so they are easier to lay your hand upon
the gun being one the glass of water the book the swan
vestas & softpack three cigarettes rough water pelliculate
notes for anonymous transfers of funds into several accounts
some light integration. And love of the watch. Intention?

Don't agree on a time a date or place best not to know
make it more of a natural deception/further apprehension
discouraged/abated with a careful observation on morality
not a 'rain clears the streets' or a 'third man' movement more
the lithe muse on extremely sharp pure speed moreover
the fascination was less with cities
tended to press a copy of Edward O. Wilson into your hand
purse the lips tight and mention biophilism as a creed worth looking into
now he can leave the room with its no-scent
into the clearing air at the end of a warm front
having passed the object over in this form/information
habitus of a life defined for you in closing
sulphate blinking on and off crisping the sleight
into brittle feints at space, ticking them off severally,
moving the blocks, running a splice through your teeth

an invitation to an event accompanied by a lack of culpability
is as rare a thing as the acceptance of history, and you don't whistle
to yourself as you leave the room and shut the door in stages
settle the account and arrive feeling weak and human somewhere

Bufflehead

The derivation of the style is not to not know it.
All introduction, like parsing a moving wave: namecheck
stamped into sand's demonstrations of beautiful affect
bending a hollow marram stalk and talking of love
were we to know it/snapped to earth. Vague curves
established over a surf decision at goose rocks beach
tremble and revert to a cline, relieved. The small matter
of a parking permit and the sleek animosity of friends
narrowed to a feral rear-guard containment called defense
backing up to the car shaking sand from the foot up.
The sufficiency of love racked back up to a broken neck
navigating the *listen y'all* back home through a japanese print
and two feet of water sweet enough to drink

Project cirrus

Some handful is creasing available leaves for selvage
and down they go as doves, seed droves, lines of familiarity

the subtle chain dropped in suspense, a cheerful task
kicking the inflationary universe 'til a bright bruise

seeks languages for code replacement, for messaging
the enemy, for making brave prediction. Where I sit

in Shaefer's icebox, breathing hard dust into snow
cat-gut as brittle inside, where the planes doth seed

with silver iodide some clouds of mountainous regions
slim ribbons of water, torn by wind, tips buoyed

by the constant bump into harm & the vertical
hand-me-down to music. Where we love this febrile mess

of vision and certitude sleek with finching
pursed & paused with sun-dogs beneath alternately rising skies

which is how we cadge a light with mountains beside us:
same excessive dream of spring, green sand and song

this is how anything creeps from information
the graph gone matte, the elegant snow brought down

to gaps in the sequence. Is falling on ether & dancing
in circles for profitable engineering. Ah, you strawberry

plants at twenty below
you indigent calm from heaven

Skipper/copper

What living creature/where the rest is pledged
to hang over a marsh in lineaments of copper
beryllium spots and a deteriorating surface
grace to call out, a few scales dropping out
leaving greasy translucent windows:
dust on the forefinger and thumb

Who cares if it flies again/flying things
dumb objects which flinch and fall again
desperate aspects are these, for to fall again
what propensity for metaphoric expression
is left? None. None. Twice a rosette blinks
holding mountains. They really are mountains.

No idiocy of quietude brings it rolling over into ice
an embellishment crackling between the same fingers
paper refuses the body but the line moves out gently
breathing almost covers the whole of the sound
pheromones motion to close or disguise closer

mottled as paper but safer, rolled
like a Hartz bird & the mouth always closed

After the war

I may be an artist, but I have gone from a baby to having the soul of a nail

Larry Rivers

In those days the air was sleek as water, and numbers like rain
breathing through glass, filling the room. Sleep the only static thing
poised a foot above the head. Glass. A sclerotic
coat, a cast: registrations of the eye and a ticking under the rasterised floor
movement of plates deeper than grief where I waited
everywhere waiting. each moment attenuated like the flutter of the paradox
just before taking breath, holding a moment to remark upon it, and then
    another:

the barometer drops to zero twice a day, as long as I have remembered
in a long series known more recently as holes in the eye of day
staring at the bar the needle drops away, an unparalleled sinecure
as if it had written itself, & I was waiting for this
to pare the days down, set them adjacent to others, ground them
in paralysis. The inclination of dreams, the whole fledged scape
stuttering, halting and not moving on. That I could thank, could be seen
as the courteousness of dreams is understood, and the function of their
    selection
sideways like wire, repeatedly tipped and replaced with wares of beauty

it was as if irony had become visible. As the air poured in, traces became
     visible
on the screen's diminution softening into number, sheet penumbrae over
     the monitor
flickering with parities & inklings of order, coiling clockwise with former
decisions marked sweetly as evolutions of favour. Some kind of diary
assuming immanence in all material objects as safety
wherein paper had been reversed, and every entry burned upon itself.
     Lightly
I replaced the book & the table was wet under the small white desk lamp's
small white pool where the air had touched, and the air was as wet
as the ink, growing wetter, blacker, more even-handed. Sleep had been
     reversed
peeling away & in panic I looked for it, and it had not been taken away.

Perhaps an inch remained beneath the plaster not yet soaked in air;
filled with an intimate flicker of flayed pressures: revealed cues
stripped. Split sticks & packets arrayed all over the sloppy terrain,
residual water burning from the arcing floor. & I was counting
one to ten, again, one to ten & this was a recognised method of achieving
     sleep
tic stammering in the left lower lid. Assume immanence in all objects,
     I said.

So I slept, shucking the pressures of particles & wire, building vision up
from ideogrammatic locii to messy cloud & attempting memory
for size, for clarity of shape, whose exact shades were resuscitation

and as the theme drifted romantically the screen breathed pure numbers
malandro est but the blade is real as bland & the sale dumped shells
half calcium and the rest mostly copper, turned by evolution or by air
whose briefest credo: the assumption of immanence in all objects
notes evolution & the pens disjecta / tierra / the sweetest line across the
    sleeve
a project initally termed a plea, but renamed as necessary

sweet as static the night curves inward
and buried deep in the fallen overpass, music:
nonplussed, holding one end of the steel nerves
spoke radio silence: inflected, the hands
registered a burr, a tiny contralto hiss in the wire
translated by wind as a local symphony: history
bleeding down the core like geographies

an indivisible score soft enough to hold in the mouth
searching itself for words, tantamount to directed speech
a stray brightness on the lip of an invasion. And knowledge of this
accorded only through outward signs, motives and lustre foiled over
home retained as a collection of maps in some relict part of the brain
desert. And the commentators, who thought snow on the cuff where it lies
questionable, holding amicable until the powder blew earthward,
and then the parrying recommence.

The defence was hybrid, and any fall, circumspect at the throat
where white feathers and sleep emerged as analogies to the brittle
chatter of my heart. To speak whatever word was required
a difficulty akin to poverty. And the hasp continually bit
until the curve of the walls sweat milk dust where the purchase
scraped psaltery in fallen plaster. Sleep's implicate rip
slewed violently west on the temperate breeze
leavened with dust and ghosted with names, one in particular
proliferating remonstrably in the dark regions cuttle-soft
where ballistics and biology both appear slightly luminous
directed as they do come from the same hands

some special utopy for the penitent stops here
splits a token fence in perfection
whose hold is readily humming a little
tune of desire, where do you breathe? nothing's obscenity but
august, tap tap

the tiny adamant whispering on
'where do I start' looking out
over the whole mild world

Gainsaid

Shot understanding right out, correctly, in a hydroptic cut/one hand
Dropping the Glock the other bowing slack outward to cinch the map
Persephone-like, with a PCMCIA faxmodem and ATM residue
Beneath the nails sugar warm plate beneath which sings
Gelatine or glass chloracne detailing the jaw touched pity by
Default coming up from Suisun city 06:30 in a hired Dodge pacific
Gulls on the flat-roofed shack saw dramamine so the eyes
Itch and the formulary cede/hedex glitters intimate as a damp wallet:
Glaucous spring wind lifts propositions & disconnections
Blamed on hardware failure the season continues wired with
Bewilderment configured/check: bland calligraphy fires news
Over on error messages thinks only where the mood takes him:
Under a dark sun wondering at tenderness and regard; under
the pass at London Bridge by way of gracious miracles JASON
Appraising his walled dead city volte-face tuning, falling
In a quick wing-over down the grid to water 'one world' put
Naphtha mutter cut-purse no matter turning the heat over and over
Like a blackout blown Kodak-flat, trading the mechanics of flight
From a paper by Pennicuik crossing the date so often, so frequently
The fibres teared out scales which eyes anyones guess the take
Glucose, anhydrous rooms, ammonia/camphor/arsenic, borax, DMSO
Patterning the skin in a sleeve of feathers and pneumatised bone
Pride dismissed. Blood from the mouth's corner. One more bruise
On the wrist. Yeah. You could foster that one out on a freeway sink,
Outwardly recogniseable; nothing to it, flat metal cocaine tang at the back
Of the throat, dark blue sunshine curving la vie moderne right out
Black cafe, parking lot. Or love it.

Monhegan

or: why I am not a painter

The option presents itself & it is the geometry of behaviour
weakness addended as lists with a curious shear from the first
whet drawn to light and hurt is blessed with a broken wrist
laws reset the amplitude and cut the bias/is what the test

in overalls, taking a flip over the board like a run/line down cadillac
erred, forgiveably, damped down with a fluster of american thrushes
weak passerines dumped in a fall on an island dripping with monarchs
no headway against an easterly wind dropping on shingle and oxidised
    wrecks

the illness is on, and the curl of shot-filled waves pronounces a dare on deck
happy as I am, ready to pan back and take in the Kent house and a roll
    up to pines
scratching some lines on a rock with a peripheral cinder is fetching
collaboration of lures I wonder. First, second, and third year gannets

distinguishable by the distribution of hues. The patch of black
falls into the open eye like the bird into surf and sets up a ratchet
mechanism the wind and land dries the cornea and the sea's
slack tangent catches you like a tune & you turn, to sleep surely

in blue and red with salt in your hair and a pin in the throat
lacking/distress as a suite of biological fitness and lax finesse
handing us on to the museum, the ice house and the light
house stilled by environmental occurrences whenever/the gut carved by
    nuance

as the merlins tip and fall into a carrying wind, scoring a sixty foot drop
    into starlings
and out into the channel below, chittering with satisfaction or annoyance
    or fear
turning to present eight toes to a conspecific rival image & the sky is
    darkening.
Where rate of change chanced to mark itself against a chevron of feathers

pushed by a proximate cause from Nova Scotia southward, eight ounces,
    six ounces, a curl

nowhere drypoint or the heel of a gull. What, here, is warmed onto palaver
by which the painter is searching for a rectangle of warm colour
linseed flat tactile slick on the instant and searching for a wall

Noar Hill

Coruscating over maize where the buff and silk and scimitar tipped contour
feather buoyed on a strong easterly passed in a second and buried deep
    in leaves

the memory of skin behind, skin and barbs walking up to the crest of
    the hill:
all he ever wished to invent was there, and that was the end of modesty

amateur light flapping on grey felt that tug to the eye like a wing bar
raw chalk and ice underfoot creased to imagine age where it soaked

gunpowder demeanour, the scent of flint and government prised
apart by frost, dropping from the sheer three foot slope as white mud

a pallor derived from deception at the window stood
bitten by river air, the roiling heart, a moment of love only

chief among these then and you are calling it in
inspiration like dry skin in its diminuition silence

and the sky is as motionless as the heart
its hook to tie it from

Earth Station

Caught the push for describing the personal and segregated it.
Remarked on it as interest in power for memory's sake, stepping out
each step discarding metaphorical intent, each print filling with water
where laminates of carbon threw steep bubbles of air & sense

to an intermediate, grave position cowled by a stack of cumulus
white *phragmites* extending thirty miles out to the far ridge
whose new dishes proliferate on unlikely chalk, child of bullet time
wading through new sedge, watching the commsat's ink-point above

constructing a beautiful personal cosmology from the inclination
of space and communicative links, where the dishes' upturned curves
represent immortality and such, so that nights long they could be watched
as the band of microwave radiation pushed up through low cloud

as ravens slope-soaring on the updraught from the dish's face some nights
in tears, drawing with greasy pen on the glass new lines between the ridge
and the point of light high above, then moving back and thinking less;
Kent sodium-dark to the east, and the sky rising to night in the west

attenuating to empyreal black and its soft dust, description:
the day breaking below vision, the arc of light
dishes half-buried in fog and the sky raising itself at dawn
static carbon on the generator exhausts & the feedlines coming in

speech in wires he laughed and returned the compliment
because they were speaking for him, as they always had done

MIR

A fragment of paint, a carrying bolt
DERA had missed & the threat of rain
so prolonged that the dictation of miracles
was abandoned. These simplicities were useless to me.
though war was all there was to see; scat and hesitancy

the brilliance of a star, the sapphire's boxed array
the cobra beside the stone & all I saw
was the nought on the scales as the snake moved, not the crowds
nor the pigeon-egg diamond in the hilt of the vizier's armory
the lock of hair or the hand of bronze to kiss

only egrets, white through lignite and soft hydrocarbons
and each wing a scant line of cartilage broken into ribs
of light and shade. Every time the line progessed like silk
iron deer, tin diamond and blue sky over Topkapi
dismembering the fortuity of travel one stop and bracketing

this was the world as it existed for our amusement
satisfactions snipped from empirical brochures entire
Ginza, Hadramaut, Nazca in six by four, milled, screened
& bleached to cuttle-ink by months of sun and wind
there are twelve, including the pyramids,

the tower in Paris, the bowed milk of the Opera
House and the silver heaped about Bilbao
the thin crenellations of a wall about hills
and the lights of a city west of an inland sea.
No distinction is offered; these are tokens only.

Your farewell is only the cuttings looking at me
their derivation is both more than ours and lessening;
the marketable and the promise of these cities both.
Either could be plain; though bells are ringing, it is only
the changes they are practising, fringes meshing into an airy

October night. And overhead a point of light travelling away
from the setting sun, the falling station describing its sere arc
before it passes behind clouds and enters the shadow of the world.

Lammergeier

Today is what either history truth maybe the civilisation of work
grandeur and its allies spread upon the long steppe

blood on their faces from the setted sun & the formes of music
chased with woodsmoke the apparell the magenta turf

single beads and microhistories & the tracts all equally torn
above the lozenged tail of the pseudo-phoenix the lambslayer's

water and golden eye, his breast feathers rusted from long contact
with oxides and bone & his long remiges comformable with pure air

his eyes abstracting rising heat from slim pillars of polarised shear
& both feet clenched as loosely as that former hand therewith nothing

but the slap of something which may once have been a standard
against the prow of white which might have been none

for there are no small pieces and the whole too large for an idea
cruising the work's reconstruction with a series of stones, markers

of the referentiality of small clearings in the merry chaturanga manoeuvre
the nervous head crested with stone and tags of water of mail

& its tiny dogtag oxides leaching into the deepening ground fragments
of a projectile recovered & loaded to be taken back home

where the long graze up to azimuth supplanted the beating heart
with the delicacy of an entirely assumed protection. What sirens.

The sparkling discomfiture of the statistician's assurance
squeaked behind the teeth & the expression of sweet brisability

which is offered in the ripple of air from the epicentre of the broken runway
in the small roses, the white cloths, and strings which disappear intire

letter to america

amid the rain of ether from the noisy sky
& the mild diffidence of dials, the drench of laws
and scripts greeting the storm, its policy of tempered
the exasperation of metals & drift as if its bloom were simple

to the corpus from below in panels, with outliers brushed into ice
the fruiting instability of air, beneath which a ribbon struggles
I am a conversation articulated quietly across oceans
regarded as a measure of uncertainty or surprise

surviving precisely as a desire for redundancy
& this morning the first the guides that lead you in
their capture/the displayed tautology the tunnels of air
preferments of fall lines, new climates tightening on the earth

waypoints for the astronaut & the arctic tern
fat crickets & car-wrecks in fine evening rain
in spilt declivities of bright symbology
tacticians drive their windward aires along

demonstrating the facilitation of flight:
the slew at sea, the captured wires & the unequal catapult
definitions too lazied to mark the precision of the first breath on deck
stepping into a rose

but you were walking towards me, after all, as if
it weren't in fact anything other than the imaginary
front sight of one index pressed to your brow
which held you to a name and its willing execution

the pure distinctions you pull upon
your eyes the specific lightness of material perfection
a static click breaking into small worlds
where death has music in a vice-like

I think not. A cloud of polarised light
the specific charade I cleave to 'miracles of' falling to machinery
one black dot spilling forwards into the brim of a pupil more distant
his schematics of rash energy, clean daguerrotypes of humidity

& humour beats down in planes and sepals from the island trees
and you say *I've dreamt this* & your voice is exceeding level
as your eyes with their perpetual ironies inquired
practically as the parable of the aviator's eye

of a shelf of clines and deteriorating greys
frayed with the packed flocks of boreal falls
nighthawks & assemblages of frosted passerines with foil legs
described as angels as the waves reflect

at ten centimeters from their mute bodies and return.
and, in the perfect meteorology of the brittle desert,
at the limit of breathable air where it thins into darkness,
these are the scripts of fallen planes, broken by fog.

& you were scraping the ice from the leading edge a.m.
printing an image of the mansions of the dead a.m.
looking for a small world in the uninhabitable air
trying to extinguish some deeper desire for fire

with something as cold and as hard and as temporary as flight
& what you were hoping is that the air would recolonise you
recognise you and welcome you into the sunlight
and all would be forgiven. ink in the thick air would curl

into glyphs of desire & the lightly starred heel
would dip into the sea at dawn as it spills
into a blaze of mute objects
in the pure suburban heavens